W9-AVN-128

EDGE
BOOKS™

SANITATION
INVESTIGATION

DO YOU KNOW WHERE YOUR WATER HAS BEEN?

The Disgusting Story Behind What You're Drinking

by KELLY REGAN BARNHILL

Consultant:
Stephen Young
Water Treatment Consultant
Winston-Salem, North Carolina

Capstone
press®
Mankato, Minnesota

Edge Books are published by Capstone Press,
151 Good Counsel Drive, P.O. Box 669, Mankato, Minnesota 56002.
www.capstonepress.com

Library of Congress Cataloging-in-Publication Data
Barnhill, Kelly Regan.
    Do you know where your water has been?: the disgusting story behind what
    you're drinking / by Kelly Regan Barnhill.
    p. cm. — (Edge books. Sanitation investigation)
    Includes bibliographical references and index.
    ISBN-13: 978-1-4296-1995-0 (hardcover)
    ISBN-10: 1-4296-1995-3 (hardcover)
    1. Water — Purification — Juvenile literature. 2. Water — Purification —
History — Juvenile literature. 3. Water-supply — Juvenile literature. I. Title. II. Series.
TD433.B37 2009
628.1 — dc22   2008000534

Summary: Describes the history of human water treatment and the current water
treatment system.

Editorial Credits
Mandy Robbins, editor; Alison Thiele, designer; Wanda Winch, photo researcher;

Photo Credits
AP Images/Arnulfo Franco, 18; Rajesh Kumar Singh, 7; Rick Bowmer, 28
Comstock Images, 4
Getty Images Inc./The Bridgeman Art Library/Hubert Robert, 12–13
Landov LLC/Boston Globe/Tom Herde, 23; MCT/Orange County Register/
    Sang H. Park, 14
Photri MicroStock/R. Bennett, 24
Shutterstock/Andrey Armyagov, cover, 1 (water); clearviewstock, 19 (road sign
    background); David Huntley, 5, 11, 15, 17, 21, 26, 29 (push pins);
    Gilmanshin, all (grunge background); Karin Lau, 27; Larisa Lofitskaya,
    19 (paper); Natthawat Wongrat, 6; Stefan Ataman, cover (faucet); Vaide
    Seskauskiene, all (cracked wall)
SuperStock, Inc./Newberry Library, 8; Steve Vidler, 10–11
UNICORN Stock Photos/Eric R. Berndt, 20

1 2 3 4 5 6 13 12 11 10 09 08

TABLE of CONTENTS

CHAPTERS

FEATURES

Chapter 1
WATERY GOODNESS

Even clear flowing water could have nasty germs living in it.

4

LEARN ABOUT:
➲ Funky floaters in your water
➲ Why your water is safe
➲ When bad water happens to good people

Nice, cool water. You can see through it, so it must be clean. Right?

Picture this scene. You're hot, sweaty, and really thirsty. Nothing could taste better than a tall, icy glass of water. Hear the clink of the ice cubes in the glass. Feel the splash of cool water on your dry tongue.

Now imagine that, floating in your water, are tiny one-celled creatures called **bacteria**. When people drink water with these germs in it, they can get sick. Really, really sick. Think diarrhea for days.

And what if, added to the germs, are rotting leaves, fish poop, dead animal bits, and garbage? Still thirsty?

EDGE FACT:

According to the Centers for Disease Control and Prevention, germs in water cause 4 billion sicknesses worldwide each year.

bacteria — small one-celled creatures found in nature; some bacteria can cause diseases.

5

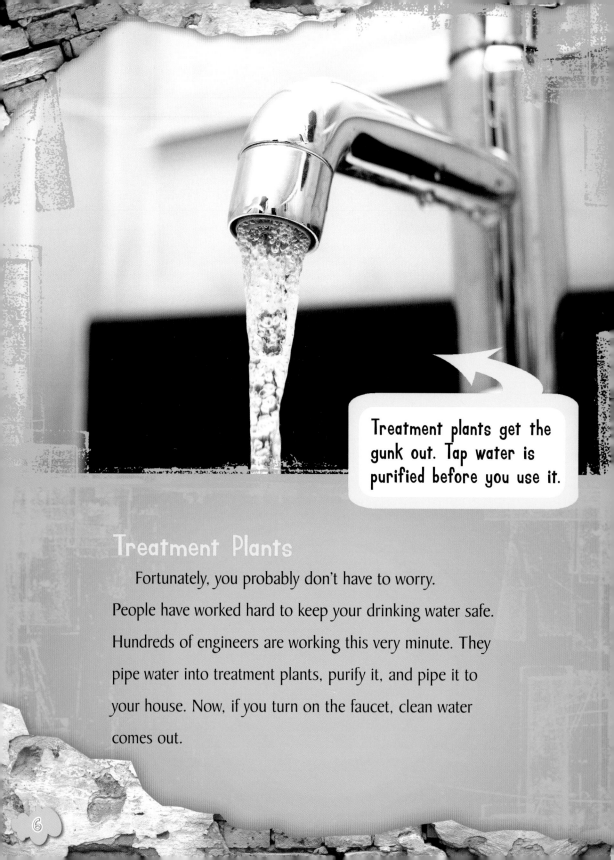

Treatment plants get the gunk out. Tap water is purified before you use it.

Treatment Plants

Fortunately, you probably don't have to worry. People have worked hard to keep your drinking water safe. Hundreds of engineers are working this very minute. They pipe water into treatment plants, purify it, and pipe it to your house. Now, if you turn on the faucet, clean water comes out.

Nasty Water Woes

The truth is, purified drinking water hasn't been around very long. For thousands of years, humans drank water that stank, tasted bad, and made them sick. In fact, in some poor countries, people still can't get clean drinking water. Yet we need water to live. Our bodies are about 60 percent water. Finding water and making it clean is important for everyone.

In many places, people have to drink water with garbage floating in it!

Chapter 2
THIRSTY PEOPLE IN HISTORY

Ancient Mayans built giant stairways to get water from underground streams.

LEARN ABOUT:
➲ Purifying water in ancient India
➲ Ancient Egyptian water filter
➲ Awesome Roman aqueducts

Since the beginning of time, humans have searched for water. Before humans built fires or shelters, they needed water to drink.

In ancient times, people didn't know about germs. But they did know that dirty water could make them sick. As the number of people on the planet grew, it became harder to bring clean water to everyone. So what did people do? They thought of new ways to clean water and bring it to people.

Intelligent Indians

Ancient people in India didn't know what germs were. But they still found a way to keep from getting sick. Ancient Indians heated water until it boiled. Then they poured it through sand and gravel. Both these techniques clean water. Boiling water kills germs, and filtering clears out other yucky stuff.

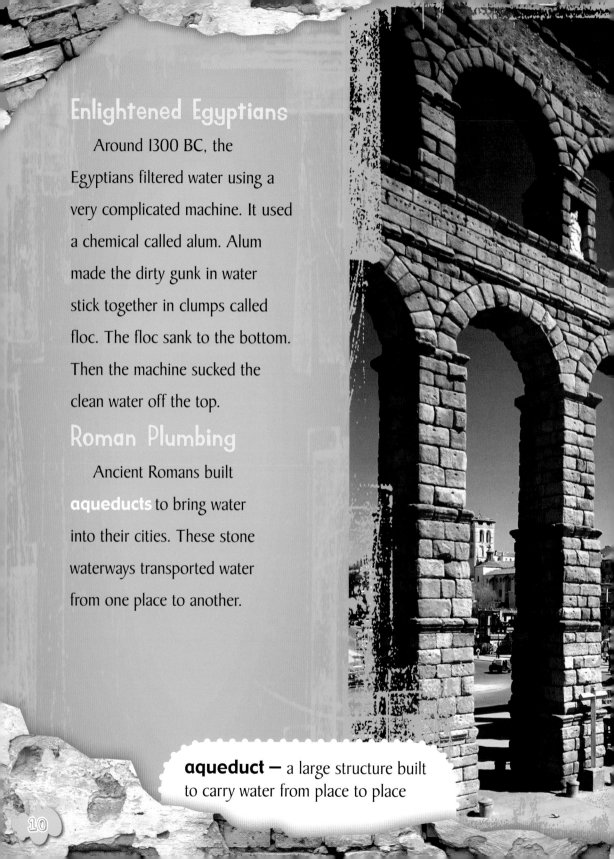

Enlightened Egyptians

Around 1300 BC, the Egyptians filtered water using a very complicated machine. It used a chemical called alum. Alum made the dirty gunk in water stick together in clumps called floc. The floc sank to the bottom. Then the machine sucked the clean water off the top.

Roman Plumbing

Ancient Romans built **aqueducts** to bring water into their cities. These stone waterways transported water from one place to another.

aqueduct — a large structure built to carry water from place to place

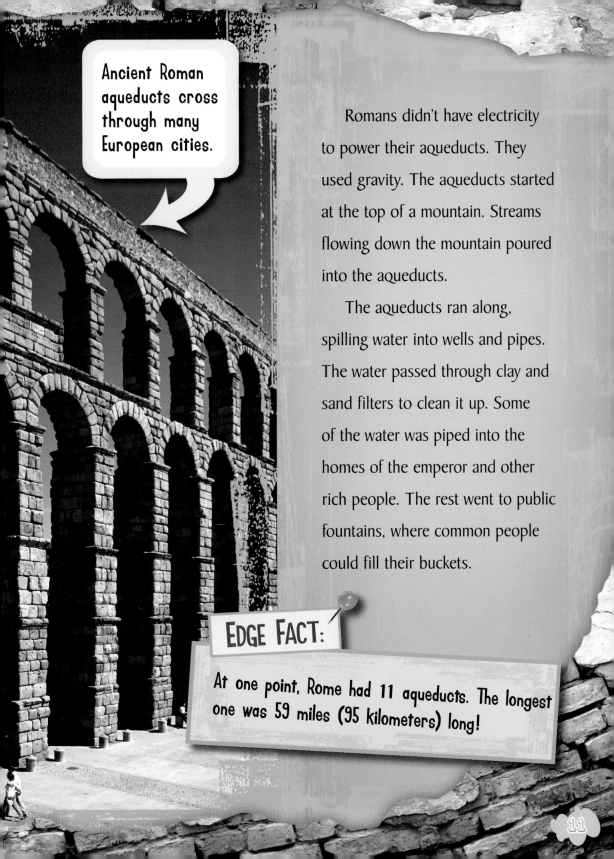

Ancient Roman aqueducts cross through many European cities.

Romans didn't have electricity to power their aqueducts. They used gravity. The aqueducts started at the top of a mountain. Streams flowing down the mountain poured into the aqueducts.

The aqueducts ran along, spilling water into wells and pipes. The water passed through clay and sand filters to clean it up. Some of the water was piped into the homes of the emperor and other rich people. The rest went to public fountains, where common people could fill their buckets.

EDGE FACT:

At one point, Rome had 11 aqueducts. The longest one was 59 miles (95 kilometers) long!

Once the Roman aqueducts were no longer usable, people used polluted, dirty river water for all their water needs.

Grimy Water Once Again

Wars broke out as time went on. The great ideas of the ancient Indians, Egyptians, and Romans disappeared once their armies were defeated.

Large sections of the Roman aqueducts were ruined during an attack on Rome. After that, Romans used water from local rivers. They also dumped garbage in them and washed their clothes and animals in them. Can you imagine drinking from a stinky, dirty river? Yuck!

Chapter 3
A DIRTY WAY TO GET CLEAN

Lab technicians make sure water is free of germs, waste, and other nasty stuff before it gets to you.

LEARN ABOUT:
➲ The "treatment train"
➲ America's water use
➲ Water waiting for you

We've learned a lot about cleaning water since ancient times. Scientists from many different fields have taught us about germs and bad chemicals. They've also discovered how to get the bad stuff out of our water. Water treatment **lab technicians** have learned the best ways to clean up water. Today, water is tested, treated, and cleaned so it's safe to drink.

There's not one single step that totally cleans water. Water goes through what's called a "treatment train." This train is a series of steps. Each step cleans water in a different way.

EDGE FACT:

About 32 percent of our drinking water is flushed down the toilet.

lab technician — a person who is trained in a specific technical process in a laboratory

15

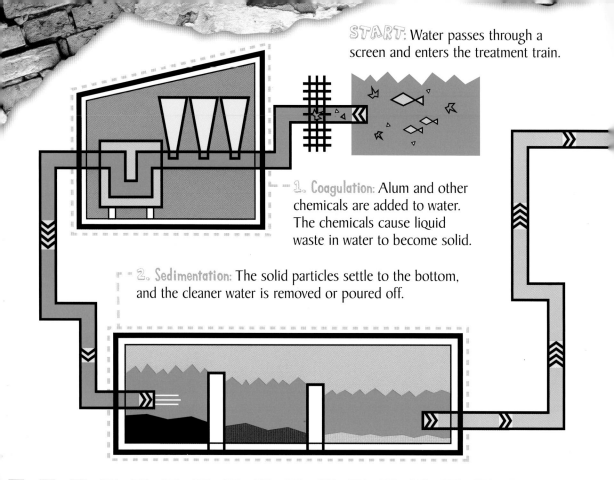

START: Water passes through a screen and enters the treatment train.

1. **Coagulation:** Alum and other chemicals are added to water. The chemicals cause liquid waste in water to become solid.

2. **Sedimentation:** The solid particles settle to the bottom, and the cleaner water is removed or poured off.

Tips From Egypt

Usually, the cleaning process starts with **coagulation**. This process was invented by ancient Egyptians. Amazingly, after thousands of years, we use the same chemical the Egyptians used — alum. Sure, we add some other chemicals to make it work better, but alum is still the main ingredient.

coagulation — a process that causes some liquids to turn to solids

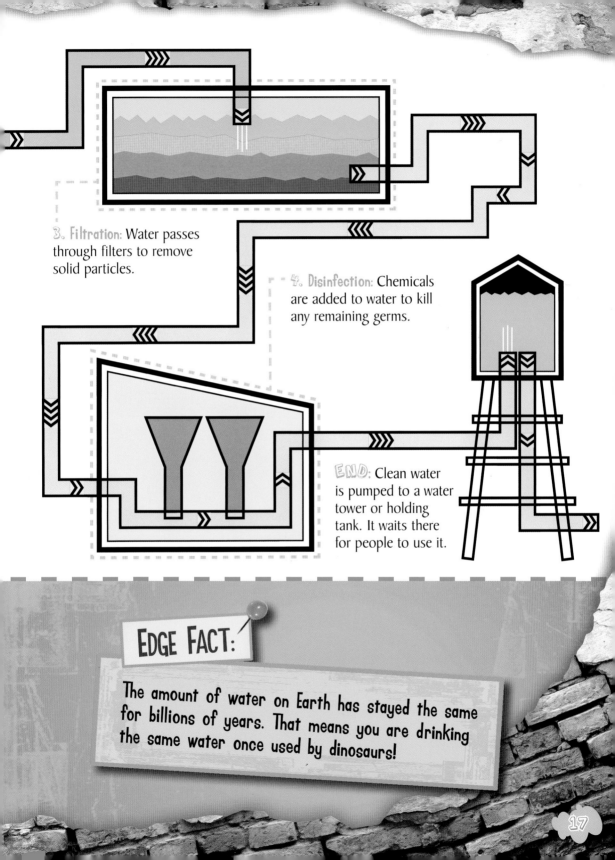

3. Filtration: Water passes through filters to remove solid particles.

4. Disinfection: Chemicals are added to water to kill any remaining germs.

END: Clean water is pumped to a water tower or holding tank. It waits there for people to use it.

EDGE FACT:

The amount of water on Earth has stayed the same for billions of years. That means you are drinking the same water once used by dinosaurs!

The people of Panama City get clean water from the Miraflores treatment plant.

Settle Down Now

Next is a process called **sedimentation**. Floc settles at the bottom and is removed, or the cleaner water is poured off. Floc from drinking water treatment plants is taken to a landfill.

sedimentation — a process in which small particles in water sink to the bottom

WHAT DO WE DO WITH ALL THAT WATER?

People in the United States use more than 402 billion gallons (1.5 trillion liters) of water per day. That's more than any other country in the world. But it's less than it once was. Luckily, we are learning to use less water. That's pretty good, because our population continues to grow. That means we have more people, but we use less water. Nice job, Americans!

So what are we doing with all that water? Power plants use 40 percent of it. Another 40 percent is used to water farmland. Factories use 7 percent. That leaves only 13 percent for daily human use. That's about 50 gallons (189 liters) of water per person, per day. How much water is that? Well, think of a bathtub. Now imagine four of them full of water. That's how much water you use each day. Think you could use less? Bet you can!

As it rides the "treatment train," water is pumped through huge tanks.

No Bacteria Allowed!

Now the water is ready for **filtration**. Water is forced through a series of filters. These filters are made out of sand, gravel, or charcoal. A filter has tiny holes that the water passes through. How small? Smaller than dirt and grime. The bacteria run into the dirt and grime left behind and get stuck in the filter. That way, we are left with clean water.

EDGE FACT:

Americans drink about 1 billion gallons (3.8 billion liters) of tap water every day.

filtration — to clean water by passing it through a filter made of sand or gravel

Chlorine Clean

The last step is **disinfection**. This process can be done in two different ways. Usually, the chemical chlorine is added to the water. Chlorine kills any remaining germs in the water. It is also used in swimming pools to keep germs from turning the water green.

Chlorine breaks down into other chemicals that are harmful to fish. Scientists think these chemicals may not be good for people, either. Some cities are now using ultraviolet light instead of chlorine. The same light waves that give us sunburns can also kill germs that make us sick. Who knew?

Lastly, water goes into storage until people need to use it. You know that big water tower with your town's name on it? That's where clean water is stored. Cities also store water in underground holding tanks.

disinfection — a process that adds chemicals to water to kill harmful germs

Would you know it if someone peed in the swimming pool? Probably not! Chlorine keeps the water from turning color.

Chapter 4

WHERE DOES THAT WATER COME FROM?

Getting clean groundwater is a dirty job. Large machines drill through layers of mud, rock, and sludge.

We use water for almost everything. We clean our houses and our bodies with it. We drink it. We flush our toilets with it. We water our crops. Without enough clean water, our cities would be dirty and stinky. The world would be filled with dead plants and very thirsty people.

What Lies Beneath

People use two kinds of water — groundwater and surface water. Groundwater comes from, well, the ground. Under the ground, to be specific. Scientists called geologists and hydrologists locate **aquifers**. People dig wells to reach aquifers. Shallow wells are around 50 feet (15 meters) deep. Bigger wells can go down 1,000 feet (305 meters) or more. The deeper the well, the cleaner the water. Why? Because for water to get down that far, it passes through lots of sand, rock, and soil. These elements filter the water on its way down. Unfortunately, you can't just replace groundwater. When it's gone, it's gone.

aquifer — an underground lake

Scratching the Surface

Surface water comes from lakes, rivers, melted snow, and reservoirs. Because surface water is open to the air, it is refilled every time it rains or snows. But it is also more likely to be polluted. Have you ever seen a flock of ducks floating in the water? Would you like to fill a glass from under those ducks and drink it? Probably not!

We also use rivers and lakes for boat travel. It's important that the water levels stay high enough to keep the boats floating. That's why communities need different sources of water. No one wants a garbage barge to run aground next to a public beach. That would stink in so many ways.

EDGE FACT:

Groundwater pumps are causing parts of California to sink. In some places, the ground sinks as much as 4 inches (10 centimeters) per year.

Clean Water Heroes

City planners and engineers work hard to find the cleanest water sources possible. They make sure that factories aren't dumping waste into reservoirs. They clean the water from the sewer system before pumping it back into rivers. They test for chemicals and poisons before the water even gets to the treatment plant.

No matter how clean a water source looks, water is not safe to drink until it's treated. That's why engineers are filtering, cleaning, and pumping water right now. Because we all get thirsty. Your city has thousands of gallons of water in underground holding tanks or water towers. It's just waiting for someone — someone like you — to turn on the tap and have a drink.

EDGE FACT:

Less than 1 percent of treated water is used for drinking or cooking.

GLOSSARY

alum (AL-uhm) — a type of crystal that helps purify water

aqueduct (AK-wuh-duhkt) — a large bridge built to carry water from a mountain into the valley

aquifer (AK-wuh-fuhr) — an underground lake

bacteria (bak-TEER-ee-uh) — one-celled, microscopic organisms that exist in and on all living things; many bacteria are useful, but some cause disease.

coagulation (koh-ag-yuh-LAY-shun) — a process that cleans water by causing some liquids to turn to solids and sink to the bottom

disinfection (dis-in-FEK-shun) — a process that kills harmful germs in water by adding chemicals to it

filtration (fil-TRAY-shun) — to clean water by passing it through a filter made of sand, gravel, or charcoal

lab technician (LAB tek-NIH-shun) — a person who is trained in a specific technical process in a laboratory

sedimentation (sed-uh-muhn-TAY-shun) — a process that cleans water by allowing small particles to sink to the bottom and be removed

READ MORE

Day, Trevor. *Water*. DK See for Yourself. New York: DK Publishing, 2007.

Fourment, Tiffany. *My Water Comes From the Mountains*. Lanham, Md.: Roberts Rinehart Publishers, 2004.

Stewart, Melissa. *The Wonders of Water*. Investigate Science. Minneapolis: Compass Point Books, 2005.

INTERNET SITES

FactHound offers a safe, fun way to find Internet sites related to this book. All of the sites on FactHound have been researched by our staff.

Here's how:
1. Visit *www.facthound.com*
2. Choose your grade level.
3. Type in this book ID **1429619953** for age-appropriate sites. You may also browse subjects by clicking on letters, or by clicking on pictures and words.
4. Click on the **Fetch It** button.

FactHound will fetch the best sites for you!

INDEX